UZR IN CONTEXT

The baseball statistics website Fangraphs.com breaks down how to understand a player's UZR this way:

DEFENSIVE ABILITY	UZR
GOLD GLOVE CALIBER	+15
GREAT	+10
ABOVE AVERAGE	+5
AVERAGE	0
BELOW AVERAGE	-5
POOR	-10
AWFUL	-15

CHAPTER 9

EARNED RUN AVERAGE

Perhaps the most dominant pitcher of all time was Pedro Martinez. Pedro thrived as a strikeout menace during the steroid era, when offense ruled (see page 12). While most players of the time were bulky and strong, Pedro stood 5 feet 11 inches and weighed only 170 pounds. Yet during his 18-year career he struck out 3,154 batters, at a rate of 10.0 per nine innings. Sometimes he fooled hitters. Sometimes he overpowered them. Either way he was dominant.

Pedro won the Cy Young Award, given to the league's best pitcher, three times, and he was the runner-up twice. But one of the easiest ways to tell how great he was is to look at his earned run average (ERA). ERA is the average number of earned runs a pitcher gives up over nine innings, the length of a game. To find a pitcher's ERA, you divide the number of earned runs allowed by the number of innings pitched and multiply by nine. (Get out your calculator!)

PEDRO MARTINEZ CAREER

919 earned runs
2827 1/3 innings
$919 \div 2827 \ 1/3 = .32504$
$0.32504 \times 9 = 2.93$ ERA

That means that for every nine innings, Pedro gave up less than three earned runs on average. In his best season, 1999, he pitched 213 1/3 innings and gave up 49 earned runs for an ERA of 2.07. The average ERA that year was nearly three runs higher, at 4.70.

TOP CAREER ERAs
Minimum of 1,000 innings pitched

Rank	Player	Team	Year	ERA
1.	ED WALSH	WHITE SOX, BRAVES	1904–1917	1.816
2.	ADDIE JOSS	NAPS, BRONCHOS	1902–1910	1.887
3.	JIM DEVLIN	GRAYS, WHITE STOCKINGS, WHITES	1873–1877	1.896
4.	JACK PFIESTER	CUBS, PIRATES	1903–1911	2.024
5.	SMOKY JOE WOOD	RED SOX, INDIANS	1908–1922	2.033

BEST SINGLE-SEASON ERAs IN HISTORY

Rank	Player	Team	ERA	Year
1.	TIM KEEFE	TROJANS	0.857	1880
2.	DUTCH LEONARD	RED SOX	0.961	1914
3.	MORDECAI BROWN	CUBS	1.038	1906
4.	BOB GIBSON	CARDINALS	1.123	1968
5.	CHRISTY MATHEWSON	GIANTS	1.144	1909

EARNED vs. UNEARNED

Runs that score due to an error by the defense are not considered "earned" by the batter, so they don't count against a pitcher's ERA.

CHAPTER 10
WHIP

◄ MARIANO RIVERA

Many faithful baseball fans today pay close attention to a pitcher's WHIP. The name stands for "walks plus hits per inning pitched." Invented in 1979 by writer and baseball fanatic Dan Okrent, WHIP is a good way to look deeper than ERA at a pitcher's performance. The stat is basically the average number of batters a pitcher allows on base per inning.

This list contains some of the greatest pitchers in history, including Yankees reliever Mariano Rivera, who retired in 2013.

▶ ADDIE JOSS

BEST CAREER WHIPS
Minimum of 1,000 innings pitched

Rank	Player	Team	Year	WHIP
1.	ADDIE JOSS	NAPS/BRONCHOS	1902–1910	0.9678
2.	ED WALSH	WHITE SOX/BRAVES	1904–1917	0.9996
3.	MARIANO RIVERA	YANKEES	1995–2013	1.0003
4.	JOHN WARD	GIANTS/GRAYS/BRIDEGROOMS/ GOTHAMS/WARD'S WONDERS	1878–1894	1.0544
5.	PEDRO MARTINEZ	RED SOX/EXPOS/METS/ DODGERS/PHILLIES	1992–2009	1.0544

RELIEF ADVANTAGE

Statistics tell us it's harder for pitchers to get batters out when they face them multiple times in a game. Batters get a little more comfortable with the pitcher each time they go to the plate. That explains the fact that relief pitchers typically have a much better WHIP than starting pitchers. Relievers face only a few batters a game, and they almost never face an entire lineup.

Of the top 10 pitchers in WHIP in 2014, only one was a starter—Clayton Kershaw of the Dodgers.

2014 WHIP LEADERS
Minimum of 60 innings pitched

Rank	Player	Team	Innings Pitched	WHIP	ERA
1.	SEAN DOOLITTLE	A'S	62.2	0.73	2.73
2.	DELLIN BETANCES	YANKEES	90.0	0.78	1.40
3.	PAT NESHEK	CARDINALS	67.1	0.79	1.87
4.	ANDREW MILLER	ORIOLES/ RED SOX	62.1	0.80	2.02
	JOE SMITH	ANGELS	74.2	0.80	1.81
6.	MICHAEL PINEDA	YANKEES	76.1	0.83	1.89
7.	BRAD BOXBERGER	RAYS	64.2	0.84	2.37
8.	WADE DAVIS	ROYALS	72.0	0.85	1.00
9.	CLAYTON KERSHAW	DODGERS	198.1	0.86	1.77
10.	MARK MELANCON	PIRATES	71.0	0.87	1.90

◄ CLAYTON KERSHAW

CHAPTER 11

FIELDING-INDEPENDENT PITCHING

Oh, those poor Detroit pitchers. On paper, the Tigers of the early 2010s had one of the best starting rotations in all baseball. But their ERA was consistently in the bottom half of the league. What happened?

Pitchers don't control everything that happens when they're pitching. Have you ever seen a pitcher get the batter to hit an easy grounder, but the infield can't turn it into an out? Some fielders are really good at making outs on balls in play. Others are not as good. Luck plays a role too.

A NEW STAT

In the late 1990s, a baseball writer named Robert "Voros" McCracken began thinking about how fans and teams evaluate pitchers. He believed that things pitchers do not control—almost everything that happens after a ball is struck by a batter—have a huge effect on scoring. To find out how good a pitcher really is, you have to strip away those things that he doesn't affect directly. McCracken wanted a stat that measures only things the pitcher can control.

In 2001 he published a ground-breaking article online in which he laid out his ideas about "defense-independent pitching" statistics. A few mainstream media members picked up on McCracken's article, including Rob Neyer of ESPN.com. Not long after that, another baseball thinker who goes by the name TangoTiger invented fielding-independent pitching (FIP).

PITCHERS' SKILLS

FIP measures a pitcher's skills based on strikeouts, walks, and home runs. Strikeouts are good. Walks and home runs are not.

FIP looks at how many of those three outcomes a pitcher allows per inning and spits out a number that looks like ERA. You can read it the same way. FIP is like a pitcher's ERA if he had received league average defense and luck.

The 2012 Detroit starting pitchers had a FIP of 3.56. That was third best in all baseball, but their ERA was 3.76. In other words, the Tigers defense was costing the team an average of .20 of a run every game. Things didn't get better the next couple years.

The Tigers' 2013 FIP of 3.12 was the best in MLB, while their 3.38 FIP in 2014 was third-best. The Tigers' ERAs in both cases were middle of the pack.

TIGERS STARTING PITCHERS

Year	FIP	ERA
2012	3.56	3.76
2013	3.12	3.44
2014	3.38	3.89

CHAPTER 12
STRIKEOUTS

Strikeouts. They're at the core of baseball. They're so important, we sing about them during the seventh inning stretch: "It's one, two, three strikes you're out!"

When a pitcher strikes out a batter, it's a show of power and dominance. He doesn't need help from his defense. The batter can't even put the ball in play.

GIVE A LITTLE, GET A LITTLE

If a hitter strikes out too often, he isn't helping his team. So hitters who strike out a lot may soon find themselves on the bench. However, there is an exception to this rule. Think about a player who hits the ball really hard. He tends to get a lot of extra-base hits, like home runs, when he does make contact. Most teams are willing to live with the strikeouts if they know the hitter will bash more homers.

Houston outfielder Chris Carter is an example of this kind of player. He struck out 182 times in 2014, but he also hit 37 bombs.

STRIKEOUT RATE

If you divide the number of times a hitter strikes out by his number of at bats, you get his strikeout rate (or K rate). Outfielder Ben Revere strikes out very rarely compared to other major leaguers. Playing for the Phillies in 2014, he whiffed only 49 times in 601 at bats, giving him a strikeout rate of about 8 percent.

◄ NOLAN RYAN

K RATE IN CONTEXT

Here's a rough guide for understanding K rates, according to the baseball stats analysts at Fangraphs.com.

EXCELLENT	10%
GREAT	12.5%
ABOVE AVERAGE	16%
AVERAGE	20%
BELOW AVERAGE	22%
POOR	25%
AWFUL	27.5%

STRIKEOUTS RISE

▼ AROLDIS CHAPMAN

In 1980, Major League teams averaged about five strikeouts per game. Today, they're averaging almost eight. One reason is that there are more hitters like Chris Carter who strike out more but also hit more homers.

Another reason is that MLB has more pitchers who can throw serious heat. Cincinnati's Aroldis Chapman has hit 105 miles per hour! As a result of his superfast fastball, he struck out a crazy 51 percent of the batters he faced in the 2014 season.

CAREER STRIKEOUT LEADERS

Rank	Player	Strikeouts
1.	NOLAN RYAN	5.714
2.	RANDY JOHNSON	4.875
3.	ROGER CLEMENS	4.672
4.	STEVE CARLTON	4.136
5.	BERT BLYLEVEN	3.701

▶ RANDY JOHNSON

SINGLE-SEASON STRIKEOUT LEADERS

Rank	Player	Team	Strikeouts	Year
1.	MATT KILROY	ORIOLES	513	1886
2.	TOAD RAMSEY	COLONELS	499	1886
3.	HUGH DAILY	BROWNS. NATIONALS	483	1884
4.	DUPEE SHAW	WOLVERINES. REDS	451	1884
5.	OLD HOSS RADBOURN	GRAYS	441	1884

STAT STARS

CAREER HOME RUNS

762, BARRY BONDS
Pirates and Giants (1986–2007)

SINGLE SEASON HOME RUNS

73, BARRY BONDS
Giants (2001)

CAREER STEALS

1,406, RICKEY HENDERSON
Athletics/Yankees/Padres/Mets/Mariners/Blue Jays/Angels/
Red Sox/Dodgers (1979–2003)

▲ BARRY BONDS

CAREER PITCHING WINS

511, CY YOUNG
Cleveland Spiders/St. Louis Perfectos/Boston Americans/
Red Sox/Cleveland Naps/Boston Rustlers (1890–1911)

SINGLE-SEASON STRIKEOUTS, PITCHING

513, MATT KILROY
Orioles (1886)

SINGLE-SEASON STRIKEOUTS, BATTING

223, MARK REYNOLDS
Diamondbacks (2009)

▲ MATT KILROY

READ MORE

Chandler, Matt. *Who's Who of Pro Baseball.* Sports Illustrated Kids: Who's Who of Pro Sports. North Mankato, Minn: Capstone Press, 2013.

The Editors of Sports Illustrated Kids. *Full Count: Top 10 Lists of Everything in Baseball.* New York: Sports Illustrated, 2012.

Wacholtz, Anthony. *The Ultimate Collection of Pro Baseball Records.* Sports Illustrated Kids: For the Record. North Mankato, Minn: Capstone Press, 2013.

INTERNET SITES

FactHound offers a safe, fun way to find Internet sites related to this book. All of the sites on FactHound have been researched by our staff.

Here's all you do:

Visit *www.facthound.com*

Type in this code: 9781491482155

Super-cool stuff! Check out projects, games and lots more at **www.capstonekids.com**

INDEX